TOAST

poems by

Anita S. Pulier

Finishing Line Press
Georgetown, Kentucky

TOAST

Publisher: Leah Huete de Maines

Editor: Christen Kincaid

Cover Art and Design: Myron Pulier

Author Photo: Myron Pulier

Order online: www.finishinglinepress.com
also available on amazon.com

Author inquiries and mail orders:
Finishing Line Press
P. O. Box 1626
Georgetown, Kentucky 40324
U. S. A.

Table of Contents

II

III

IV

For M E G J W C G L

You know who you are

I

Pandemic Erasure

Poetry that survives strategic erasures reminds me:
what is missing reveals what remains.

I am not many things
not black
not a believer
not young
not patient
not forgiving
not bi-lingual
definitely not Republican,
no scientist
no mathematician,
certainly no philosopher

but I have been to Wonderland,
heard Alice's warning—
No use going back to yesterday. I was a different person then.
So I intend to erase a bit here and there.

Call it poetic license or a life well lived,
I don't give a damn.

■

Sceptic's Aubade

*We should look inward and think about the meaning of our life
and its purposes, lest we do it in 20 or 30 years and it's too late.*
—Robert Coles

Every morning a mockingbird sings outside my window. I strain to catch the lyrics. Overnight the world has carried on without me. In this early morning light every creature is performing an intricate routine. The spider is eating insects snared by its web, the birds are rejoicing at the ripe berries. Why then does morning light seem so unforgiving? Is it that bare truth reveals its jagged edges in twilight? I crawl out of bed fully awake and feel the earth tremble ahead of the day. Must I think about the meaning of my life and its purposes now, this very morning? I have so much to do, so many places to be and when I shut my eyes to begin the task of reckoning the sunlight is blinding.

Illusive Truth

Speaking on NBC's "Meet the Press," Kellyanne Conway said White House press secretary Sean Spicer's false claims about crowd sizes at the inauguration were "alternative facts."
Jan 22, 2017

Trust Merriam,
burrow into
pages worn thin,
pass by Alternative,
pass B, pass C,
pause at D: Decency,

screech to a stop at F,
linger on Fact,

skip to T—reclaim Truth,
apologize to no one,
rip the page out,
paste it on your heart.

■

7th Inning Stretch

Love stories
buried in clichés
inch from brambles,

prickles, once brittle,
now surprisingly soft,
twist easily into metaphor.

Even wild passion has a shelf life,
and after its "use by" date
morphs into comfort.

Weary of desperation it changes
pace, is affable, accommodating.
What was once demanding waits its turn,

redefining the game,
tip-toeing past Go, rejecting
the very concept of winning or losing.

■

Ars Poetica Sans Hammer

Art is not a mirror held up to reality but a hammer with which to shape it.
—Bertolt Brecht

I am pressing pen against paper
humming a catchy tune—
still, my poem remains a poem.

Words trapped in verse,
dependent on the line before,
the line after,
the line break between.

Sure I hear the loud demands
of an impatient muse
dangling reality like a savory treat

while issuing the same nasty warning
time is short get to the point,
which of course I already knew.

I pick up the pace,
sharpen the words,
line them up on the cliff's icy edge.

If pushed will they soar,
reshape a random bit of starlight
or hook up with space junk on a journey of missed opportunities?

■

Soundtrack

*The mirror brims with brightness; a bumblebee has entered the room
and bumps against the ceiling. Everything is as it should be, nothing
will ever change, nobody will ever die.*
—Vladimir Nabokov

The dryer tosses old clothes washed thin
the computer clicks and flashes
the radiator pipes bang rhythmically

while the frantic buzzing of a fly
trapped in 13E on the Upper West Side
evokes seasons of green meadows

when spring unleashed
buried us in riches, now
this desperate buzz transports me,

and under the glaring light of verse,
days long gone reappear,
ageless.

■

Exactly What Is Victoria's Secret?

Victoria's lacy bras and G-strings
adorn naked mannequins behind
grimy windows on Broadway and 86th.

The local orthodox complain. In time
displays of female parts in delicate lingerie
become commonplace, the pious learn to rush by.

Recently, in the middle of winter, a homeless man
wrapped himself in heavy blankets
and lay beneath Victoria's female wannabes.

Playing Russian Roulette with wind, ice and snow,
he claimed his ground as shoppers
paraded past and stepped around.

Today, as light snow fell, sunlight bounced off
those frigid dummies onto his sausage-wrapped body,
and I wondered if Victoria's frilly bras and panties

seduced, aroused or just confirmed
what he has known so long, that
the road home is often hopelessly convoluted.

■

Meditation

I ask him to join me in learning how to meditate from my new app.

Why, he says.

So you can clear your mind.

It's clear, he says.

So you can avoid the distractions that muddle things.

I am almost never distracted, he answers, puzzled.

Please, I need you to help me meditate.

How? he asks.

Maybe if you sit with me.
Sit with you?

Well, when I am alone I hear you in the next room.
I think about what you are doing. I wonder what you are thinking,
if you are happy or hungry or tired.

And when I don't hear you moving or clicking computer keys
I assume you are dead and I plan my widowhood,
which does not seem to achieve the goal of meditation.

Not surprised, he says laughing.

■

If It's Not One Thing...

Lewis Thomas, the renowned physician, poet and essayist said, "The great secret of doctors, known only to their wives, but still hidden from the public, is that most things get better by themselves; most things, in fact, are better in the morning."

The ache in my back has passed
but my shoulder is making a strange
creaking noise when I roll over in bed

which is when I notice
that you are not beside me
and see the hall light shining
through the crack in the bottom of the door

and when you finally return to bed,
quietly slipping in beside me
I am fully awake and gently slide

out of the jumbled covers
noticing that the pain in my back
has returned and has moved to my hip.

Although many years a doctor's wife
I am riddled with doubt as the
unflappable daylight flirts

with the remnants of evening
running the clock down on
the moments left to heal.

■

Survival

As I recall it was a beautiful Sunday. We arrived at the Bronx Zoo
with two small kids screaming from the back seat. Amid the tumult
I saw in your face a yearning for the unencumbered life, freedom to
ingest a quiet contemplative world. Instead, there we were, at the
zoo, kids barely glancing at the elephants, uninterested in the tigers,
chasing after pigeons. It's not that much of a story: exhausted young
parents juggling noisy toddlers more interested in street birds than
exotic wildlife. I wonder if you recall that day and others like it?
Days when we found ourselves ensnared by plans doomed to fail.
Days we kept a death grip on all we held dear by ignoring caged
beasts, surrendering to the unexpected.

■

Weather Report

My husband is in the next room
yelling at his new Google phone.
This phone responds only to his voice.

I, who never scold Siri
sit helplessly as he barks
into the air insisting

on a weather report
to decide if he needs a sweater
before we go out.

He used to rely on me to decide
if he should wear a sweater.
He used to look out the window.

I attempt to graciously
accept the seasonal demands of
my beloved's eccentric routines.

I do wonder, if the disembodied voice
on his Google phone informs him that
it is freezing, snowing, hailing or sleeting

on what is clearly a lovely Spring day,
will this retired gray haired physician,
this ardent scientist, become a keening acolyte,

ignore the empirical evidence
of sunlight streaming
through our Upper West Side windows?

But I, who have learned
to pick my fights,
wait patiently.

Ultimately he will
choose me over technology,
take my hand,

and together we will elevator out
into this gorgeous April day
breathing in the certainty of renewal.

■

Anniversary

After years of celebrations
affection became predictable
even tedious,
we were fueled by it but
too busy to notice,
involved in the cycles,
the details of daily life, with
little time for reflection.

And then on an ordinary sunlit afternoon,
(the kind of afternoon in which
we stop preparing lunch
to ask each other the day and date)
you simply turned your graying head
and looked at me.

I wondered who you saw.
Was it someone you once knew,
someone no longer available?

But in the fullness of that glance,
fear became gratitude,
lunch a celebration.

■

The Sin of Omission

Valentines, anniversary cards,
lined up in the market next to
heart shaped chocolates,
scream of undying love.

Have you noticed that
things have morphed,
what was trite
seems surprisingly apt?

My love,
put your silver mane
on my shoulder, touch me,
and as I read to you

of nightingales, rainbows
and bleeding hearts,
do not raise your brows,
giggle or snort.

Coursing through years
rich with savvy days
I fear certain words
may have gone unsaid.

■

II

Plan B

Before the moon no longer intrigues

before pill bottles clutter the windowsill

before seeing rain as a hazard

and seasons a marker of loss

gather the thorny issues of aging

squeeze them until they squeal

and in an arrogant huff

turn up the non-digital volume

on music from the sixties

take a delicious moment to wallow

unclench your calloused fists

allow this poem to assure you

that answers to every one

of your unspoken questions

will make you dizzy with joy

■

Seeing the Light

*Fireflies Have a Mating Problem: The Lights Are Always On… It's getting
harder for them to reproduce because light pollution is outshining their
mating signals.*
—*The New York Times*, Feb 3, 2020

Joycie and I gripped empty jam jars
with pin punctured silver foil caps
to catch fireflies.

We put bits of grass inside
believing we were
creating a splendid home.

By morning they were dead,
jars discarded by parents
as we went off to school.

Tonight, as I watch their descendants
flitting about in the dark,
flashing split seconds of light,

I wonder how many years
it takes to understand
that home is an idea,

not a place, and
if you get it wrong
it can kill you.

■

Memo to Hospital Maintenance

For four days I have studied
the crunched up sandwich wrapper
and empty soda can hiding under
the worn plastic couch

I have glanced repeatedly
at the huge clock
on the cracked peeling wall
that insists it is 12:30

I have stared out of grimy windows
to the bustling street at a world that
does not know that he is almost gone

At a time when nothing is clear
this room announces in clipped tones
that one has entered a realm of no joy

I would advise management
not to change a thing
no repainting
no magazines

and respectfully request
that the old sandwich wrapper
and empty soda can
remain under the left corner
of the green plastic couch

I would argue
that this foul room
is a peculiar sanctuary
where 12:30 defines both
evening or morning

Spiritual Sceptic

Our handsome monk
sported a round bald head
and orange flowing robes.

Anxious to please we sat
in cross-legged silence,
offering a clear ready mind,

earnest in our search for
an uncluttered version
of our daily selves,

but we were visitors,
awkwardly folded
on the temple floor,

struggling
to reach that inner peace
which might keep us from wondering

why, in a place where materialism is rejected,
was everything in the temple
covered in gold?

■

Interspecies Meddling

Early morning stroll. I stand back against the gritty wall of a pre-war building to watch a small bird frantically zipping back and forth, over and over, through the narrow canyon that is 98th Street, gracefully weaving between parked cars, landing momentarily on the air conditioner of the bagel store, flying over building canopies and garbage cans. Little bird, I ask, what's up? There is a whole city to explore. Why limit your flight plan to 98th Street between West End Ave and Broadway? There are two magnificent rivers on the shores of Manhattan, there are five boroughs, hundreds of thousands of streets, hills and valleys, millions of trees in full summer bloom to call home. Listen, all this drama is foolish. Are you using this fluttery search to make a point about something lost, something irretrievable? Point taken. Move on.

■

Inside Out

Slower and gray,
COVID tags us *most vulnerable,*
abruptly shuts us in.

Desperate to keep everything alive
I have over-watered the cactus.

He focuses on the kitchen sponge
where lurking viruses hide,

and so we fuss and worry
until a soaring cello
transforms the room
with the power of Bach

unleashing memories of
a world no longer accessible:
the Parthenon, Sistine Chapel,
Mona Lisa's savvy smile,

teasing me
into believing that
if I keep close watch
over the drowning cactus
we will both survive.

■

Mea Culpa

We suffer more often in imagination than in reality.
—Seneca, *Letters from a Stoic*

Define catastrophizer...

a solo traveler on an endless
journey to the edge,
wary of inner peace, of stoicism.

An involuntary devotee
of the uncentered,
paying homage
to rich dark possibilities.

One whose over-examined life
is always a split second away from
fabulous freakish doom desperately
held at bay only by perceptual readiness.

One who, sharing the vantage point of raptors,
takes note of the gullies and sheer rocky cliffs
disguised as daily life, who smiles and nods

at well intentioned hecklers advising
relax, live in the moment,
while out of the corner of her eye keeps
vigilant watch on the ravenous tiger circling
everyone she has ever loved.

■

Rolling the Dice

I skip past
UNICEF
NOW
Planned Parenthood
J Street
The ACLU
The DNC
Bernie and Elizabeth
Earthquake and hurricane relief,

open only
holiday greetings
celebrating the Jewish New Year,
an invitation to cast off sin
with kith and kin at the beach.

Still, the weeping world is insistent,
oozes through cyberspace and
drowns out the trumpeting shofar.

There I am, stranded, sandwiched
between the seasonal rituals of an ancient
holiday and others' jarring pain.

I nod to the god
I do not believe in,
propose a deal:

keep everyone I love safe and
I will grapple with despair and failure tomorrow.

Today I will nurture joy
and unfounded optimism,
eat apples and honey,
celebrate the tribe.

■

Pandemic Reality Show

Another quarantined morning
weather irrelevant—
she walks into her closet,
inhales stale scents and
with the power of a fairytale kiss
wakes a dormant dress,
gingerly removes it from a dusty hanger,
decides to revive one neglected outfit
every quarantined day, smooths
the silk dress, lays it out on her bed,
showers, combs her greying hair,
puts on makeup, earrings, wraps
her mother's ancient pearl necklace
around her neck, grabs her phone,
snaps a selfie, smiles at an aging woman
wearing her favorite blue silk
deftly redefining a shapeless day.
Allowing the silk to caress her,
she stares out the bedroom window
at the cloudless blue sky, hits send.

■

You OK?

In this quarantine marathon
morning is evening.
Hours poorly punctuated
like a run-on sentence
suffer from adjective flooding

long
frightening
sad
sunny
dreary
endless

Innocent verbs
face the danger
of domestic abuse

wake
cook
sleep
shower
wash
eat

eyeglasses steam up over masks
droplets swarm like summer's no-see-ums.

April arrives
cherry trees bloom
daffodils sparkle in exhaust free air
mockingbirds imitate screaming sirens.

How small the difference
between noise and song.

My love, look up!
The sun rises and sets
the faint moon promises
OK?

Damn,

we may have missed it,

the split-second friendship migrated
across an entrenched familial border,

when DNA was silenced, overruled.
Listen!

Ancestors whisper from the grave
this is good they say,

definitions of family
desperately need updating,

your world can be so new,
welcome it.

■

A Life Re-imagined

… fiction makes a better job of the truth.
—D. Lessing

Doris Lessing
re-wrote her mother.

Took a life lived
and substituted

a pen and ink mother,

one she imagines
she might have loved

one that might have loved her.

The rest of us
focus on conjugating verbs,

the mothers we had,
the mothers we should have had,

the mothers we have been,
the mothers we should have been,

hoping that in sum
the picture will not require

a re-write.

■

Questions

Texas Church Turned into a Memorial After Mass Shooting
—CNN, Nov. 13, 2017

Is the mind's eye a universe?
Can angels repel rapid fire?
Are devils redeemable?
Have we reversed down with up,
throwing off our celestial GPS?
How does forgiveness fit in?
What's the cutoff date?
Do the dead tire of eternity?
What is optimism in the absence of breath?
Can hope survive machine gun fire?
Will country crafted wooden pews
wash clean after soaking in an ocean of blood?
Is suffering preordained?
That neighbor who bent over to grab her fallen bible—
and survived...
how exactly was that choice made?
Details, please.
Oh, yes, and
are the newly dead able to clean the slate?
What about the kids,
who did not yet have a slate to clean?
Does pain like this remain forever fresh?
Is eternity akin to infinity?

For god's sake
Prayers and thoughts,
were never the issue.

■

Obituary Math

Despite a lifetime of humanities courses,
I have become an expert
in the mathematics of death.

Like Bridey Murphy, one day I woke up fluent,
subtracted the start date,
from the end date,

skimmed the compacted life story, noted the
survivors casually listed in the last paragraph,
focused on the numbers,

the genetics, the probabilities of prediction.
Mrs. Green, my fourth-grade teacher, whose obit I missed,
would have been pleased with my proficiency,

even though I suspect she knew then,
as I do now, that when it comes to the fear of loss,
simply getting the numbers right is worthless.

■

Stepping Out

How do you know but ev'ry bird that cuts the airy way,
Is an immense world of delight, clos'd by your senses five?
—William Blake, *The Marriage of Heaven and Hell*

A red-tailed hawk swoops down
penetrating slivered city canyons
and their distorted shadows.

Piles of clear plastic bags stuffed with trash
provide color and background
as vast hinged wings sail the updraft.

But why is this bird on West 98th Street
and not in the wilderness?
Is it drawn by the stench of garbage or
the romance of a life lived in stacks?

People rush by
immune to the stench,
the soaring bird,
the chopped-up pieces of sun.

I point one finger at the sky
so you will see,
so we both can see.

We have missed so much,
failing to look up.

■

The Last Word

A plague arrives toting death.
What was a body now renamed corpse,
dead a close relative of alive.

My small diamond necklace and wedding band
heirlooms not yet delivered.
My pallid face and stiffening frame

a disposal problem for a few burly,
mindless masked mortuary handlers
tasked to find a spot to park me, unimpressed

by the bits and pieces of me that
I have painstakingly tucked
into a few rigorously revised poems,

ensuring that even without eyes,
ears or breath I will live forever,
assuming, of course,
that somewhere there is a reader.

◼

Snared by the Net

When those alluring lights first seduced us
we scrambled aboard, signed in,
allowed ourselves to be shackled to a screen.

Virtual and physical
arteries congealed,
seasons changed without notice.

We, who were taught how to parse a sentence,
obediently hit *LOL* or *like*
on keys so close and small they seem to kiss.

Now, the bloom is off,
even that pompous GPS
can't find us in the fetid fog of viral infection.

Enslaved, we continue
to push *send*. Are we
hoping to be heard or rescued?

■

I forgot to tell you

there was a huge translucent beetle on our deck
stuck on its back, wings and legs flapping
hysterically in an attempt to flip over.

Afraid to use my hands
I went to get the broom,
but the phone rang and by the time

I got back it was gone.
Did it finally right itself, fly off?
Did a bird swoop down and eat it?

Had my fear of touching it
doomed it or was it lucky
that things resolved before
I caused any harm?

That's how it is so often.
I struggle not knowing
when to stand by,
when to jump in.

Not sure why I am telling you
about this now, days later, but
I believe it's important
that you know I get it.

∎

Failed Reunion

Picture this... two teenagers
whose high school survival
depended on each other

fall out of touch,
let years pass before
re-connecting

but before they re-unite
someone posts a digital message
with the word accident, the word died.

Now, daily, I see her everywhere,
in the diner,
in the concert hall,

in the market,
bouncing that head of ruler-straight blond hair
that crooked smile

I knew at 17
how I will know her forever,
which as it turned out
was not all that long.

■

Check-up

It's my mind's eye
I say to the weary doctor,

Can you sort me out?
My children have aged,

my love
sports grey,

lines once sharp
shimmer colorless.

In the mirror an unfamiliar woman
blocks my view.

I shoo her away but
she does not appear to scare easily,

seems stunned.
Please, Dr., it is the end of March,

Spring and Summer tease.
She so wants to be ready.

■

Snapshots

Incomplete memories compete,
frozen faces poke out of old shoe boxes,
yellowed snap shots wriggle loose from worn albums,
disgruntled after years of captivity
in the hodgepodge stew of an unsorted past.

My gentle mother
hair rolled like a Twenties movie star
grins into the camera
and Dad, tall and handsome,
stands beside her, my fifth birthday cake
aloft, raised sky high in triumphant arms.

Tempering melancholy with affection
I resign myself to what will be
a messy legacy of echoes,

pin my hopes
on help from the digital world
offering perfect order
on a wafting cloud.

Order unobtainable
here on earth.

■

Notes of a Party Planner

(Your presence is requested to celebrate the Mayan Apocalypse)

The end of the world may be tomorrow
but at this moment I am still here
and I have little time to plan
order a caterer
a clown
a preacher
gather the family for the final farewell or
the survival gala

and what an odd celebration it will be
Beethoven and Mozart
Bruce Springsteen and Elvis
Shakespeare and Yeats
Martin Luther King jr and Abraham Lincoln
Picasso and Michelangelo

gathered in a hand holding circle
spanning the globe as it spins into oblivion
swaying to the rhythm of a collective heartbeat
balancing the power of myth
with the glory and shame of what we once were
or, if calculations are a bit off,
on what it is still possible for us to become

■

III

Stanley's Layers

Memo re: "The Layers" by Stanley Kunitz

Stanley advised, "Live in the layers not on the litter,"
but he is gone.

Whom then to ask about
the crusted rings on the shelves of the empty fridge,
the trash smelling of coffee grounds,

the crumpled bed linens tossed into mountains of sexual debris,
the light bulbs sizzled and popped,
the laundry languishing in the dryer,

and what to do about
that death grip on melancholy for
whatever was loved but is forever lost?

Surely the layers are the place to be,
massaging ideas into insights, examining,
meandering, exploring.

Still, I wonder who dealt
with Stanley's litter so that he might rise
above the dense debris of daily living

to poetic exaltation, and whoever
it was, was there time left

to relish and explore
the layers and all they had to offer
or is there a risk that once

that cushion of litter is gone
fragile layers may be
jagged edged

and just too difficult to navigate.

■

Housekeeping

Art washes away from the soul the dust of everyday life.
—Pablo Picasso

Sticky, thick and ephemeral,
sweep, dust, vacuum.
We remain coated in it.

Dig, toss, catch as
a flash of insight from
a stranger's right-brain

transforms the ordinary into

something indefinable,
something stunning,
something you may regret,

something that
once exposed
refuses denial.

■

Jammed

I

Two blocks
from the ocean,
vacant sidewalks,
empty zebra crossings.
Growing old behind the wheel.

Jammed—
so near the Pacific.
Idling metal
spewing exhaust,
unable to reach you.

II

Consider abandoning
the car, envious,
imagining you admiring
the streaky sunset,
hearing the tides crash.

III

Texts appear, where R U,
amid vibrations created by
basso drum beats escaping a neighboring car.

The sky darkens,
I sway to the pulsing beat,
recall your awkwardness when we dance.

So many years together,
still stepping on each others' toes.

■

Thanks But No Thanks

I tap my foot to find level ground
as though I were blind
but I am not
just slowing down
confidence shaken
by pundits trumpeting
adamant gospel on achieving
serenity and the oft touted
wisdom of old age.

I'd rather hunker down with poetry
in a place where promise thrives
in concert with the demands of age.

A place where one can
grapple with loss,
celebrate love and
embrace resistance,
while wallowing in the heartbreaking joy
of growing old in iambic pentameter.

■

Red Diaper Babies

In Jewish Harlem legs grew faster
than budgets, immigrant mothers
relied on knickers and knee-highs
worn thin until shins shone through.

Like a tale from Dickens, weary women,
grieving the loss of the old country,
trudged off daily to sew "garments" in hot workshops.

Hebrew lessons, bar mitzvah training,
stews left for neighbors to heat,
long dark hallways, communal toilets,
defined childhoods of struggle.

Dad, an inventive boy
sells soda in Central Park,
spends hours in the library, grows
tall and lean, excels in school,

holds down part-time jobs
channels anger,
joins the Young Socialists League,
the American Labor Party,

stands on soap boxes bellowing
his message, convinced there is a better way.
Law degree in hand,
he takes a stab at the good life,

falls in love,
marries well, buys a house,
drives a Cadillac, runs for Congress
on the American Labor Party ticket,

The USSR fails,
China disappoints,
he gets old,
his hair turns grey,

and his kids,
rapt and loyal followers,
learn to layer idol
worship with skepticism.

But, oh how I miss those impassioned lectures,
the comfort of that voice,
that fierce conviction, and mourn the lost
chance to jettison doubt and wholeheartedly climb on board.

■

Workaday

Not yet allowed to cross the street
I waited patiently at the corner,
peering down the block, until he appeared
walking home from the F train.

I, who have
traveled the world,
seen many wonders,
believe that no
wilderness trek,
no safari thrill,
has ever compared
to the moment I would spot him,
my five-year-old heart racing,
small frame bouncing up and down,
waving, screaming Daddy, Daddy,

and he would laugh,
drop his briefcase,
lift me high above the world,
challenge me to guess
which sweaty palm held
a piece of bubblegum
or penny candy.

Oblivious to his
long and burdensome day,
I long assumed that my joy,
my earth shaking happiness,
was all that consumed us both.

■

This Joint is Hoppin'

(Ode to Recovery)

I allow a man dressed in scrubs
and a team of masked strangers
to saw me out of Momma's framework
and replace her handiwork
with flying buttresses.

After the assault I spend weeks
incorporating alien machinery,
enduring the irritating
gospel of full recovery and

dwell on a persistent longing
to reassure Mom, long gone,
that the essence of me,
the girl she raised,
remains intact.

How splendid,
to finally embrace
that illusive acceptance of change,
the freedom to swing
marvelous man-made hips
to an unfamiliar syncopated beat
and call it a dance.

■

Fat Free

The carefully coiffed model on the TV screen
is using a metal tool to peel layers off
a clay sculpture of a naked women.

She grins
shaving off thin pieces of clay as
a male voice-over promises

that you too
can be altered until
finally flawless.

His basso voice
assures middle of the night viewers
that your mother will never know

the child she painstakingly
nurtured dislikes
so much about herself.

The Voice says nothing about
what lies ahead, nothing about
despair, self-love,

or the bruising truth
about casual
bedroom intrusions.

I flip the channel
take a deep breath,
worry about
the weary women
still tuned in.

■

The Lesson

I tilt my small frame from side to side
hunting for smooth air,
searching for balance.

I feel my father's steady support
as he grips the seat and runs alongside.
Inexplicably something clicks

and Dad, once a fatherless child
who grew up bikeless, releases his grip.
I am on my own.

Later, in triumph, he confesses:
never learned to ride a bike,
never been on one.

I file this information
for future processing
allowing that small girl

to stay focused on adoration
of an omnipotent father who repeatedly
ignored fear of the unknown.

Now, I risk awakening
dormant grief to recall
the beloved Schwinn,

the colored streamers on the handlebars,
the lessons learned
far beyond the task at hand.

■

My friend,

I know how this works.

When the funeral din has passed
ashes scattered, food gone
stories told and re-told
the world transformed by absence
objects once familiar
now threaten as
you lean into the silence
searching for relief,

even her
beat up broom
rests at a disloyal tilt
perfectly willing to sweep
for younger
less gnarled hands.

And there you are,
sinking into her body
creases in the worn fabric
of her ancient sofa
believing you
will never see
beyond the gaping
hole of her absence.

Finally on an ordinary day
with a million chores undone
you will take a walk
in a blooming garden
and you will be unwilling
to miss another second.

And that is when
this journey will have been completed
in the sloppy way any journey is completed
when you don't really have a destination

■

Act Three

A finite change of perspective
clears the clutter.
Every ounce of strength
every bit of compassion
every resource
earned or imitated
now called up.
Unconditional love,
total adoration,
unqualified admiration
gone with him forever.
The role of daughter
makes unimaginably
difficult demands even
after it is over, knowing
we must now teach the children
how this is done
so they will be ready
for their turn.

■

GPS Malfunction

Starting point—
hips, shoulders, knees,
oil leak, funky engine.

Destination—
mechanics, doctors,
garages, hospitals.

Let's go.

Watch out!
Swerve,
avoid WebMD,
debris on roadway.

Kowtow to
clocks springing forward,
clocks falling back,
road narrowing, black ice,
thinning bones, tiny blood clots.

Hazards. Hazards.

Wave to familiar faces.
Everyone you know
is on this road.

When the robot
texts, "driver?" lie,
hit "no, passenger,
attempting to navigate",

keep your cool,
request alternate routes,
time of arrival.

■

Staying Grounded

The Natural History Museum
has on its digital display
a black button-down
biodegradable burial suit.

None of cremation's
grisly boney bits,
no coffins or embalming.

Kiss your loved one goodbye,
wriggle those lifeless limbs
into the suit, button up,
toss into rich deep soil.

Add nothing.
No marker,
no stone, no flag.

Allow
the living essence
of what was lost

to penetrate your days,
sorrow to invade your gut,
grief to color your nights,

but oh, when you are able,
breathe, re-focus on
the greening world.

You will be amazed
at everything still alive,
nurtured, beautiful.

■

The House

The house remains untouched.
I know its every crevice,
its secrets,
its stashes.

I see my father's worn chair,
his cello resting on its side,
his black glasses open on the piano,
The Family of Man book on the living room shelf.

Though leveled long ago,
the house refuses to succumb.
My tulle prom dress hangs in the upstairs closet,
the crayoned flower blooms beneath the kitchen table,

the hallway staircase, down which I waltzed on my wedding day,
lures me into an endless labyrinth, stumbling over
the clutter of this richly endowed museum,
struggling to clear a path to nurture the dead.

■

Aunt Freda's Secret

Spinster—
nasty word
sharp enough to cause terrible injury.

But we nieces and nephews
never thought of her that way.
She was ours, always there

at every occasion,
every holiday,
part of us.

We were fully grown
with kids of our own
when her cancer arrived,
Death not far off, bedridden,
she waved me in,
whispered,

I want you to know
I had a lover
for many years
I was loved by him,
loved him.

Years of surmise raced by as
this death bed gift
charted a new trajectory,
filled in blank spaces,
altered sorrow.

■

Shopping With My Father

I follow his directions.
We arrive at a storage unit
in a seedy neighborhood,
a "Sale" sign propped against
a rickety folding chair.

Dad and I are the only customers.
Inside the bin are dozens
of mass-produced Chinese violins,
cellos, violas, bows and cases, leaning
against the tin wall. All dirt cheap.

We are intrigued:
the mystery,
the number of instruments,
the shady surroundings.

Dad, age 92,
a chamber music fanatic,
an amateur cellist, is enthralled,
ready to harvest this ripe fruit.
He announces he will buy
one instrument for each
of his great grandchildren.

He hondles with the owner,
they strike a deal, he
buys child sized cellos
violins, bows, and cases.

I remind him that the great grand kids
are very small.
He raises his eyebrows at the interruption.

I adjust, embrace his mission,
perhaps his last shot
at influencing children
who would soon know him
only from stories and photos,

and perhaps
in these instruments
he envisioned a legacy,
a chance to transfer a dream
about immortality
and a Beethoven sonata.

■

Dining Out

Have you dined with us before?
the handsome young waiter asks.

No, I answer.
Are you excited?

Excited? about what? dinner?
I answer:
Lets try interested,
curious, hungry, or pleased.

Will this feedback distract the Chef?
Will he oversalt the soup,
overcook the pasta,
underwhip the cream,
carelessly debone the fish?

I bring to this table
a lifetime of meals prepared
for children and grandchildren,
for this man beside me gone grey,
for aging parents ashes scattered,

and to every meal rich memories
of rushing from work
to set a table, fold napkins, arrange cutlery,
broil, bake, and roast while
worshiping the god of family dinners,
desperate to invoke
the promise of storybook endings,
despite knowing that the kids
had pizza on the way home from school.

Excited? Not really,
but pleased.
Think the Chef will accept pleased?

■

Blessing from Behind

Long run is a misleading guide to current affairs.
In the long run we are all dead.
—John Maynard Keynes

Runners, symbols posted on their chests,
struggle towards an ever illusive finish.
I bring up the rear.

My feet sink deep into the rich earth
made thick with layers of doubt, I
trudge along breathless.

Ahead each has chosen a leader to break the wind:
Pope, Guru, Rebbe, Imam, Mufti,
Evangelist, Priest, Minister.

Each dons a kippah, burka, tallis,
rosary, headscarf and hair shirt
to weather the demands of obeisance.

Each waves to bystanders, spews
enthused noisy claims
to ultimate wisdom.

Despite aging, despite loss,
I never have
joined ranks so there I am

bringing up the rear,
nurturing angst,
lagging further and further behind,

repeatedly checking my watch
while muttering about
this tiresome knotty quest for an alibi
even before a crime has been committed.

■

IV

Septuagenarian Aubade

She finds the missing creamer
in the freezer.
It does not belong there.

In the insistent early morning silence she
sips her watery tea, assures
herself she is aging well,

googles dementia,
takes a weary breath,
rises to greet the dawn,

after all, anything misplaced
in the harsh tundra of her freezer
can be defrosted or replaced,

unlike this sunrise,
unlike this day.

■

Dear MAGAs

There are more things in heaven and earth,
Horatio, than are dreamt of in your philosophy.
—William Shakespeare

What's missing is the welcome,
the worry, the asking, the hesitation
to inflict irreparable damage.

What's missing is the listening,
the hearing, the ingesting
the Other's story.

What's missing is the raised eyebrow,
the rejection of weaponized prayer
fueled by hate and anger.

What's missing is the nod
to Earth's feverish future,
the grief of broken promises.

What's missing is an apology,
the agonized regret,
the elasticity of empathy.

What's missing is vulnerability,
the failure to fear a charred
barren planet.

What's missing is the poetry.
Every atom belonging to me
as good belongs to you.

Oh yes, and joy.
Joy is missing.

■

Citizens United

Charged words—
Founding Fathers, Constitution,
Democracy, Voting Rights—

spouted by SuperPacs
to skew outcomes,
fuse, split, and upend process,

baptize the Big Players
in rivers of cash-stained
holy water,

make sure those
without photo ID and alligator shirts
are turned away at the polls.

And Justice?
She roams hallowed halls,
head bowed,

scales tipped,
pacing, moaning,
muttering something
about love of country.

■

Patience

Negative space distorts,
fills in empty,
cozies up to
what's not there,
embraces the void,
a grimace, a diabolical poker face,
muffles unintelligible words
all swept together yet kept apart.

There's a trick to flipping this.
Brush aside academic wisdom,
focus on coincidence,
happenstance, luck, serendipity.
Rely on irrational optimism, grit.

■

Mazel Tov

I hardly knew the friend of a friend
next to me at the lavish bar mitzvah.

She leaned in and whispered
how upset she was to be losing her pubic hair.

I do not recall the Torah selection
that triggered her attack of melancholy.

Her teary eyes and somber demeanor
probably appeared to the congregants

as deep admiration for the
decoding of ancient wisdom

in this ritual celebration of adulthood,
but in fact this aging beauty,

overly made-up,
jingled her gold bracelets and lamented

the far-reaching consequences
of a hairless crotch, offering

a different perspective on coming of age.

■

Virtual Nest

For E and G

I know how to cut and paste.

This skill, acquired late in life,
allows me to forward articles from
a variety of journals and newspapers
to my grown children

whom, I suspect,
rarely open them.
I remain undaunted.

How else to keep them safe
remind them to exercise,
get a colonoscopy,
have their teeth cleaned?

Hiding behind the work
of respected journalists
I nurture the delusion
that I am simply a conduit
passing on vital information,

despite knowing what
my kids have known for years:
that I have miserably failed
to cap the angst of motherhood
to keep everyone I love perfectly
safe, always.

Miraculously,
my sons have mastered the
fine art of simultaneously loving,
ignoring and carrying on, as I
cut and paste,
hit send.

Poor Adrianna

I am worried about Adrianna.
For months the same e-mail
appears in my spam
several times a day it calls, "Hey You."

Poor Adrianna,
the same "Hey You" for months,
have you no literary aspirations?

Darling Adrianna,
Are you sitting in that infamous Internet cafe
in Russia, Afghanistan, Mozambique or Tanzania

or are you right here in the USA,
full beard and hairy chest, large hands
nursing a beer patiently waiting for my reply?

Sweet Adrianna,
rest assured
this rejection is not personal.

Do not despair,
although I may trash
your daily missives

I send best regards
across oceans
riding electronic airwaves of distrust.

■

Why John of God Can't Cure You

Not because he's a fraud
or will cut your skin in strange spots
or squeeze your head while uttering
nonsense

but while he is cutting
squeezing and uttering
you will see
only his face
feel only his hands

and miss
the spinning orb on which
the rest of us are balancing
with our palms turned up
outstretched towards you

■

Elegy for Alice

In our twenties when the world was laced with choices
taunting us to map the perfect life, we grabbed
our two small kids left NYC and went to live in London.

In the iconic basement dining room
of our St. John's Wood home
I set the table with the landlady's fine china,

dunked teabags into a porcelain teapot,
filled cream pitchers and sugar bowls, placed
small fruity British cakes on an antique dining table.

I remembered you, Alice.
How hard could a tea party be?

Guests arrived,
How interesting, one said holding her cup aloft,
tea in the consomme cups.

Yes, I answered, surprised at the two little handles.
That's how we do it at home.
And she nodded politely,

said the tea is lovely.
Thank you, I answered smiling,
hoping the little paper tags on the

Lipton tea bags would not float to the surface and
unmask me, a very young woman
who had never been to a tea party

and assumed the absence of the Mad Hatter
was achievement enough if one
relied on a stiff upper lip, kept calm and carried on.

■

If You See Something Say Something

(Sandy Hook)

I see the pinking sky
the cluttered earth
the leapfrogging children

the frost on the rotting pumpkin
kindergarteners cowering
flowers on tiny graves

I see the crush of bullets
the idiocy of arms
the scattered debris of limbs

the giddy distorted
rush of a soaring bullet
the whiplash speed of loss

the stinking breath of anger
the still pools of grief
shame I see shame

I probably should say something
but what?

■

Septic System Emergency

The moon refuses
to wax or wane,
tides barely
reach the shore,
gravity struggles to pull.

His gut, thick with
foie gras and Big Macs
clogs an aging system.

By early morning
exhausted,
seriously backed up,
vile tweets seep out.

We turn our befouled flag
upside down.

Take the plunge
embrace the movement,

Resist.

■

9 AM on the 96th Street Crosstown Bus

9 AM on the 96th Street Crosstown bus. Talkative 4-year-old girl sits
    next to me. I smile at her. She starts chatting, asking all kinds of
    questions: *do I have kids, where I am going, what I am doing.* I
    answer as simply and appropriately as I can.

Finally, almost at Lexington Ave where I get off she asks if I have a father.

No, I answer, *I had a father but he died years ago.*

Shot? she asks authoritatively.

No, I answer, *he was very old and died of old age.*

Old age, she echoes, puzzled, *died of old age?*

Yes, I say waving goodbye, wondering what just happened.

■

Holiday Spirits

Saturday morning fire at London Zoo leaves one aardvark missing.
　　　　　　　　　　　　　　　—*Sky News*, December 23, 2017

Pig nosed and small footed,
ripped from an African home
to a London petting zoo.

Perhaps the flames
evoked dormant bravery,
allowing this aardvark
to find a crack in the system,

relying on sheer terror to
waddle away from the searing flames,
burrow to a pub,
order a pint,
celebrate freedom.

In the optimistic version
of this Holiday Story,
the aardvark organizes
sympathetic pub crawlers,
returns to free its comrades,
and, forces joined,
the rebels do whatever it takes
to make meaningful change
for the New Year.

■

Take My Advice

Do not affect a breezy style; use orthodox spelling; do not explain too much; avoid fancy words; do not take shortcuts at the cost of clarity; prefer the standard to the offbeat; make sure the reader knows who is speaking; do not use dialect; revise and rewrite.
—E. B. White

Hey, it's me
me
a bit fogged-in
altered, older,
still re-examining
in from out
up from down
seriously
this is no joke
propagating
(red line that word—too many syllables)
or spreading ideas
if you reduce them (red line that one as well)
to nonsense ... get it?
Are you listening?
Paying attention?
Ready to sweat?
Good.
Now I will do whatever
I must to ignore
all this wisdom
carry on

■

Ode to Our Freezer

I admire its chill
unsung ability
to preserve the status quo ante,

To redefine perishable,
accept preservation not
immortality as the goal.

Even the thaw
a surprising opportunity
offering the gift of perspective.

And last night
on a midnight foray
into our kitchen

We stood
before our empty fridge,
jet lagged, weary, welcomed

home by the low-pitched
hum of the deep freeze reminding us
of all we have so painstakingly stored.

■

Essentials

Beneath the mandatory mask
the air is warm and moist
like recycled grief, tedious, inescapable.

I am steeped in the myriad rules
of a viral quarantine,
negotiating the labyrinth
of penetrable borders.

Gulping fetid masked air
while dreaming of lift off,
I am flapping arm-wings,

on my way to market
desperate to ingest the air of
some distant unearthly paradise.

But I am no angelic seeker
of inner peace, no spiritual devotee,
it's the messy cacophony I long for.

Arriving home
laden with survival nutrition
I unmask, pay resigned homage
to the misshapen beloved
here and now.

■

Celebrating Evolution

You emailed your nephew about four hours ago—nothing,
texted your grandson two days ago—nothing,
sent the NY Times a letter to the editor brilliantly
zeroing in on the GOP's behavior—not even a formal rejection.

Clearly, Anita, relevance is eluding you.
Men no longer turn their heads when you enter a room.
Breasts are hanging low.
Your arguments too vehement,
jokes missing the mark.

Why then are you so at ease?
Content to stare the bullies down,
excuse the kids their slow responses,
raise a middle finger to the haters?

This woman, Anita, this one,
is surely more fun to share a life with,
accepts rejections and criticisms with a shrug,
keeps insults alive on the back burner just for the hell of it.

It's a strange twist.
Attitudes, challenges,
now easier to dissect,
less worthy of angst.

Is Carpe Diem,
once idiomatic nonsense,
now on top of the re-shuffled deck?

Look at you,
concentrating on the sunset,
on the way he still looks at you,
as though amused, casually
wraps an arm around you,
and night after night,
points out Venus, and Jupiter
lighting up the sky.

■

Acknowledgements

A Moment in Time—*riverbabble*
Aunt Freda's Secret—*The Emma Press Anthology of Aunts*
Check-up—*Verse-Virtual*
Damn,...—*Spillway*
Dear MAGAs—*Cultural Weekly*
Dining Out—*Your Daily Poem*
Failed Reunion—*riverbabble*
GPS Malfunction—*Juniper*
Housekeeping—*Sounds of Morning*
Inside Out—*Red Fez*
Jammed—*Gyroscope Review*
Memo to Hospital Maintenance—*Perfect Diet*
My friend,...—*riverbabble*
Ode to Our Freezer—*Your Daily Poem*
Sceptic's Aubade—*Spillway*
Staying Grounded—*Red Fez*
The House—*Good Reads*
The Lesson—*Silver Birch Press*
Toast—*Askew Poetry Journal, Perfect Diet, The Legal Studies Poetry
        Anthology, The Butcher's Diamond*
Virtual Nest—*Your Daily Poem*
Weather Report—*Is It Hot In Here Or Is It Just Me?: Women over forty
        write on aging*
Workaday—*Juniper*
You OK?—*Writing in a Woman's Voice*

Anita S. Pulier has a BA in English Literature from New York University and a JD from New York Law School. Anita practiced law in a unique firm in New York and New Jersey with her father and two brothers. Anita also served as a U. S. United Nations representative for the Women's International League for Peace and Freedom.

After retiring from her law practice, Anita traded legal writing for poetry. She and her husband Myron now split their time between the Upper West Side and Los Angeles.

Anita's book *The Butcher's Diamond* and her chapbooks *Perfect Diet, The Lovely Mundane* and *Sounds of Morning* are published by Finishing Line Press. Several of her poems have been featured on *The Writer's Almanac* broadcast and have appeared online and in print in many journals as well as in six print anthologies: *Grabbing the Apple*, the poetry edition of *The Legal Studies Forum*, *The Emma Press Anthology of Aunts, The Poeming Pigeon: In the News, Psalms of Cinder and Salt*, and *Is It Hot In Here Or Is It Just Me?*

Anita's website at http://psymeet.com/anitaspulier/ includes video interpretations of some of her poems.

www.ingramcontent.com/pod-product-compliance
Lightning Source LLC
Chambersburg PA
CBHW021152090426
42740CB00008B/1056